ANIMALS GROWING UP™

HOW KANGAROOS GROW UP

Heather Moore Niver

Enslow Publishing
101 W. 23rd Street
Suite 240
New York, NY 10011
USA

enslow.com

WORDS TO KNOW

developed Having grown to a certain size.

hind At the back; for example, hind legs.

joey A baby kangaroo.

mammal An animal that has a backbone and hair; females usually gives birth to live babies and produce milk to feed their young.

marsupial A mammal that carries and nurses her young in a pouch on her belly until the babies are fully developed. Kangaroos, opossums, and koalas are marsupials.

nurse To feed a baby milk produced from the body.

nutrients Materials that provide what a body needs to grow and live.

teat The part of the body from which baby mammals nurse.

waste Pee and poop.

CONTENTS

AMAZING MARSUPIALS

Kangaroos are bouncy mammals with a little something special. It's a pouch! This pouch is a special fold of skin that only females have. Baby kangaroos live inside these cozy pouches for the first few months of their lives.

FAST FACT

A mammal with a pouch is called a **marsupial**.

A mother kangaroo carries her baby in her pouch.

BOUNCING BABY KANGAROO

Mother kangaroos only carry their young for twenty-one to thirty-eight days. The baby kangaroo, called a joey, is less than one inch (2½ centimeters) long when it is born!

Kangaroos are only found in Australia.

A newborn joey is pink and hairless.

POUCH LIFE

When the joey is born, it crawls up into its mother's pouch. It is not completely **developed** yet. It lives in the pouch for months.

A newborn joey is safe and warm in its mother's pouch until it gets bigger.

9

NURSING

The mother has to nurse her new baby. The joey attaches to her teat. The tiny joey cannot even swallow. She pumps milk into her baby's throat using her muscles.

FAST FACT

The joey feeds on its mother's milk nonstop.

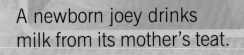

A newborn joey drinks milk from its mother's teat.

HOUSECLEANING

When the joey is tiny, the pouch soaks up its waste. The mother sometimes has to clean out her pouch. She sticks her snout in and licks it clean.

A joey can stay in its mother's pouch while she cleans it.

FAST FACT

A wallaby is smaller than a kangaroo, but it is in the same family.

CROWDED HOUSE

An older joey may still spend time in its mother's pouch when a new one is born. The mother makes two kinds of milk with different nutrients for each baby.

FAST FACT

A group of kangaroos is called a troop, herd, or mob.

An older joey nurses from its mother. The herd looks out for danger.

LEAVING THE POUCH

After a few weeks, a joey can let go of its mother's teat. It starts to spend time outside of the pouch. It can start eating grass like the adults.

A joey eats grass.

FAST FACT

Joeys usually leave the pouch for good after seven to ten months.

JUMPING JOEY

Kangaroos are powerful jumpers! Strong hind legs and tails and big feet help them jump as far as 30 feet (9 meters)! They can move more than 30 miles (48 kilometers) per hour!

Kangaroos can swim, but they cannot walk backward!

A joey's legs and tail help it jump high.

TALE OF A TAIL

The kangaroo's tail helps it balance while it jumps. Kangaroos also balance on their tails while they kick with their hind feet.

FAST FACT

Young kangaroos play-fight to practice for adult life in the wild.

Two young kangaroos play-fight. One balances on its tail to kick.

FAST GROWERS

Female kangaroos are full grown by fourteen to twenty months, and males are grown by two to four years. The largest of the kangaroos might be more than 6 feet (2 meters) tall!

A female is called a doe, jill, or roo.
A male is called a buck, jack, or boomer.

Someday, this small joey will grow up to be as tall and strong as the big buck next to him!

23

LEARN MORE

Books

Davin, Rose. *Kangaroos*. North Mankato, MN: Capstone Press, 2017.

Franks, Katie. *Kangaroos*. New York, NY: PowerKids Press, 2014.

Leigh, Anna. *Meet a Baby Kangaroo*. Minneapolis, MN: Lerner Publications, 2017.

Websites

Easy Science for Kids

easyscienceforkids.com/all-about-kangaroos

Learn more about kangaroos with videos, vocabulary, facts, and much more.

National Geographic Kids: Kangaroo

kids.nationalgeographic.com/animals/kangaroo/#kangaroo-hopping.jpg

Check out facts and photos of kangaroos.

INDEX

Published in 2019 by Enslow Publishing, LLC.
101 W. 23rd Street, Suite 240, New York, NY 10011

Copyright © 2019 by Enslow Publishing, LLC.

Library of Congress Cataloging-in-Publication Data

Names: Niver, Heather Moore, author.
Title: How kangaroos grow up / Heather Moore Niver.
Description: New York, NY : Enslow Publishing, 2019. | Series: Animals growing up | Includes bibliographical references and index. | Audience: Grades K to 3.
Identifiers: LCCN 2017045218| ISBN 9780766096479 (library bound) | ISBN 9780766096486 (pbk.) | ISBN 9780766096493 (6 pack)
Subjects: LCSH: Kangaroos—Development—Juvenile literature. | Kangaroos—Infancy—Juvenile literature.
Classification: LCC QL737.M35 N58 2017 | DDC 599.2/21392—dc23
LC record available at https://lccn.loc.gov/2017045218

Printed in the United States of America

Photos Credits: Cover, p. 1 Jami Tarris/Corbis Documentary/Getty Images; pp. 4-23 (background image), 15 Stephanie McIsaac/Shutterstock.com; p. 5 K.A.Willis/Shutterstock.com; pp. 7, 9 Roland Seitre/Minden Pictures/Getty Images; p. 11 Mitsuaki Iwago/Minden Pictures/Getty Images; p. 13 B. G. Thomson/Science Source; p. 17 SA Tourist/Shutterstock.com; p. 19 Theo Allofs/Minden Pictures/Getty Images; p. 21 Sebastian Kennerknecht/Minden Pictures/Getty Images; p. 23 John Carnemolla/Shutterstock.com.